AI Automation
for SMBs

A brief introduction to using AI automation for small and medium-sized businesses

AI Automation for SMBs

A brief introduction to using AI automation for small and medium-sized businesses

In today's ever-evolving business landscape, harnessing the power of technology is key to gaining a competitive edge. AI automation stands as one of the most impactful technological advancements in recent history, offering you the potential to substantially cut costs, save time, and elevate your operations and quality to new heights.

For many small and medium business (SMB) owners, "AI automation" might sound daunting, suggesting that it's a resource exclusive to large corporations. This guide is here to dispel that myth, revealing how AI automation is not only accessible but can also be a critical asset for businesses of any size.

We'll take you through understanding the basics of AI automation to identifying processes in your enterprise that are ripe for automation. We'll showcase use-cases from various industries, illustrating the tangible benefits businesses have reaped from embracing automation.

This introduction is meant to empower you to take the lead. We'll provide you with practical advice for pinpointing inefficiencies in your business operations and offer step-by-step directions for embarking on your automation journey. You'll discover how to capitalize on automation opportunities that yield immediate and significant long-term benefits.

Understanding that each business's approach to automation is unique, we explore how to tailor automation solutions to fit your specific needs. This includes deciding when to consult external experts and how to select the right partners or tools for your automation projects. By the end of this guide, you'll have the knowledge to make educated decisions about incorporating AI automation into your business.

We also recognize the challenges and concerns you may have about adopting new technologies. We'll tackle common misconceptions about AI automation, address potential hurdles, and offer strategies to overcome them. Our goal is to ensure that you feel confident and prepared to enter the world of AI automation.

The strategies and tips provided are designed to be actionable and relevant, building a strong foundation for your future initiatives.

By integrating AI automation, you're investing in more than just technology—you're investing in your business's future. The efficiencies and insights gained from automation will free up time and resources, enabling you to focus on what you do best: innovating, growing your business, and serving your customers.

This introduction is designed for all levels of experience, from eager novices to skeptics of AI. It's time to learn how it may benefit your company, and set out on a path of expansion and profitability.

Let's begin.

Chapter 1:

What is AI Automation?

In the arena of contemporary business, "AI automation" is a term that is gaining momentum, signifying a new epoch of productivity and ingenuity. But what does it actually entail? Essentially, AI automation involves integrating artificial intelligence (AI) technologies into business processes to execute tasks normally requiring human intellect. These tasks can vary from analyzing extensive datasets to making predictions or interpreting and responding to human speech.

AI automation is not about supplanting human workers; it's about enhancing human capabilities, enabling more efficient business operations and allowing employees to dedicate time to strategic, imaginative tasks. It's a strategic tool that, when utilized wisely, can transmute monotonous, repetitive tasks into automated operations, thus freeing up invaluable time and resources.

The Mechanics of AI Automation

To fully comprehend AI automation, it's vital to dissect its two key elements: artificial intelligence and automation. Artificial intelligence involves simulating human intelligence in machines designed to think and act like humans. When a machine displays characteristics affiliated with the human mind, such as learning and problem-solving, it is recognized as AI.

Automation, by contrast, refers to the execution of processes or procedures with minimal human intervention. It functions based on set rules and instructions and lacks inherent intelligence. However, by infusing automation with AI, an impressive synergy is created that can learn, adapt, and make decisions, thus elevating the basic concept of automation to a more dynamic and potent level.

Applications of AI Automation

AI automation is revolutionizing various sectors, redefining how tasks are conducted. In customer service, AI-powered chatbots can manage numerous inquiries at once, offering immediate responses that direct customers to resolutions, thereby improving the customer experience and lightening the load on human employees.

In the realm of marketing, AI automation enables businesses to analyze consumer behavior, crafting personalized strategies that engage the ideal audience with the appropriate message at the opportune moment. In finance, AI automation refines processes such as fraud detection and risk assessment, yielding quicker, more precise analyses and hence fortifying security and operational efficiency.

The Benefits of AI Automation

The merits of AI automation are extensive. It offers scalability, allowing businesses to accommodate growing operations without a corresponding increase in overhead. It boosts accuracy by diminishing human errors in routine tasks. Furthermore, it provides actionable insights obtained from data analysis, assisting in decision-making and strategic planning.

AI automation also democratizes efficiency, rendering advanced technological capabilities available to businesses of all scales.

Embracing AI Automation

For businesses ready to embrace AI automation, the journey starts with recognizing its potential and pinpointing areas ripe for transformation within their operations. Integrating AI automation enables businesses to not only refine their processes but also discover new avenues for growth and innovation.

In summary, AI automation marks a transformative leap in business operations, delivering a powerful combination of efficiency, accuracy, and intelligence. As we venture further into this age of technological progress, AI automation emerges as a symbol of advancement, heralding a future where businesses can flourish with amplified capabilities, adaptability, and competitive edge.

Chapter 2:

The Impact of AI Automation on SMBs

Embracing AI in Small and Medium-Sized Businesses

AI automation is more than a buzzword in the realm of small and medium-sized businesses (SMBs); it's a catalyst for efficiency, innovation, and growth. Across diverse industries, SMBs utilize AI to redefine operations, enhance customer experiences, and secure competitive edges. We'll highlight some real-world examples showcasing AI automation's tangible benefits within the SMB landscape.

Retail Revolutionized

A small outdoor apparel retailer tackled inventory challenges and improved customer service using AI. By adopting an AI-powered inventory management system, the business accurately forecasted demand, optimized stock levels, and minimized waste. Introducing an AI chatbot on their website provided round-the-clock support, answering inquiries, recommending products, and aiding in orders, which improved customer satisfaction and reduced support costs.

Hospitality with a Personal Touch

Boutique hotel chain personalized guest experiences and operations with AI. They implemented an AI-based CRM system that analyzed guest data to offer custom recommendations and services. Guests received personalized suggestions from the AI system, while AI automation optimized the hotel's internal operations. This led to increased guest satisfaction, repeat business, and enhanced revenue.

Manufacturing with Precision

A custom auto parts manufacturer incorporated AI to refine production and quality control. AI-driven predictive maintenance predicted machinery issues, reducing downtime and repair costs. AI-powered quality control systems ensured product quality and consistency, elevating precision and efficiency, which secured larger contracts and improved market position.

Professional Services Streamlined

An SMB-focused legal services provider transformed operations using AI for document analysis and legal research. AI tools expedited document processing and information extraction, while AI-powered legal research tools provided comprehensive case preparation insights, enhancing service robustness and efficiency.

Marketing with Insight

An eco-friendly products e-commerce startup leveraged AI analytics to analyze consumer data and optimize marketing strategies. AI-driven insights informed targeted campaigns and personalized communications, while AI automation supported dynamic pricing and inventory adjustments, boosting conversion rates, customer retention, and profitability.

The Common Thread

These industry-spanning success stories underscore a central theme: strategic AI automation can help SMBs surpass traditional limits, bolster core strengths, and achieve extraordinary results. AI has enabled improvements in customer engagement, operations optimization, and innovation.

For SMB owners, these narratives are an invitation to explore AI automation's potential as a transformative asset. By pinpointing processes ripe for automation and choosing the right AI solutions, your business can start a journey toward enhanced efficiency, superior service quality, and enduring growth.

In forthcoming chapters, we'll explore how to identify automation opportunities and implement AI in your business. The experiences of these thriving SMBs offer lessons and insights to guide your AI automation journey.

Navigating the AI Automation Landscape in SMBs

Integrating AI automation into small and medium-sized businesses (SMBs) is an exciting journey, offering a wealth of opportunities. However, it also comes with its share of challenges. Knowing these challenges and how to address them is crucial for SMBs eager to leverage AI effectively. Here we will outline common hurdles along with practical solutions for SMBs to successfully implement AI automation.

Challenge 1: Understanding AI Automation

The complexity of AI can be daunting, leading SMB owners to hesitate in adopting these technologies.

Solution: Education is essential. SMB owners should engage with webinars, online courses, and industry literature to learn about AI. Case studies and success stories, especially those within their industry, can clarify AI's applicability and benefits. Workshops and consultations with AI experts can also demystify AI and help tailor it to specific business needs.

Challenge 2: Cost Concerns

Perceived high costs can deter SMBs with tight budgets from implementing AI solutions.

Solution: Begin with automating a few key processes that promise immediate benefits and ROI. Look for AI tools with scalable pricing and consider the long-term financial benefits, not just the upfront costs.

Challenge 3: Fear of Disruption

New technologies can disrupt workflows, and staff may worry about job security or adapting to new systems.

Solution: Maintain open communication with your team, involve them in the process, and ensure they understand that AI is designed to augment their roles, not replace them. Provide training and support to facilitate a smooth transition.

Challenge 4: Data Privacy and Security

As data reliance increases, navigating privacy laws and breach risks becomes more complex.

Solution: Choose AI solutions that meet industry standards and regulations. Establish strong data governance policies and train your team in data security best practices. Keep your security measures up-to-date to protect customer trust.

Challenge 5: Selecting the Right AI Tools

The vast array of AI tools and services can overwhelm SMB owners.

Solution: Clearly outline your business needs and goals before exploring AI tools. Solicit industry recommendations and opt for tools with a strong track record. Testing solutions during trial periods can help ensure a good fit before full commitment.

Challenge 6: Integration Issues

Integrating AI tools with existing systems can be complicated if those systems are outdated or incompatible.

Solution: Audit your current technology to identify integration issues. Partner with AI providers that support integration or hire IT consultants to ensure a smooth process. Upgrading legacy systems might be necessary to reap AI's full benefits.

Challenge 7: AI System Maintenance

Ongoing maintenance and updates are necessary to keep AI systems effective, a potential strain for SMBs without IT teams.

Solution: Select AI solutions backed by excellent customer support and maintenance services. Stay up-to-date on system maintenance best practices and consider partnering with an IT service provider for ongoing support.

Challenge 8: Measuring ROI and Impact

Assessing the impact of AI automation can be tricky, complicating investment justification and future tech decisions.

Solution: Set clear metrics and benchmarks before AI implementation to effectively measure impact. Continuously evaluate these metrics to gauge performance and refine your AI strategy, ensuring you can communicate AI's value to stakeholders.

SMBs that understand these challenges and apply thoughtful strategies can effectively navigate AI automation's complexities and tap into its full potential for business success. The path to AI integration is an endurance race, requiring patience, perseverance, and a proactive stance toward overcoming hurdles, setting your SMB up for sustained growth in the AI era.

Demystifying AI Automation for SMBs

The world of AI automation is rife with myths that can deter small and medium-sized business (SMB) owners from embracing this transformative technology. Dispelling these myths is crucial for informed decision-making and for leveraging AI to its full potential. Let's address these common misconceptions and reveal the truths that can empower SMBs on their AI journeys.

Myth 1: AI is for Big Corporations Only

Reality: AI automation is not just for large companies. Many AI tools are tailored for SMBs, offering scalable and affordable solutions that can automate tasks across various business functions, helping small businesses to compete effectively.

Myth 2: AI Will Eliminate Jobs

Reality: AI automation aims to augment human work, not replace it. By taking over routine tasks, it allows employees to engage in more meaningful work, potentially enhancing job satisfaction and innovation.

Myth 3: You Need Coding Skills for AI Implementation

Reality: Many AI tools are user-friendly, requiring no coding skills. They feature intuitive interfaces and provide strong customer support, enabling non-technical SMB owners to adopt AI.

Myth 4: AI is Too Expensive

Reality: The cost of AI automation has decreased over time. Flexible pricing models make AI accessible for SMBs, and the ROI from increased efficiency and customer satisfaction can be significant.

Myth 5: AI Runs Completely on Autopilot

Reality: AI requires oversight. It needs regular monitoring and updates to ensure it meets the evolving needs of a business and remains effective.

Myth 6: AI Lacks Personalization

Reality: AI can actually enhance personalization. It can process vast data sets to provide tailored recommendations and services, often outperforming human capabilities in efficiency and accuracy.

Myth 7: AI Results are Instant

Reality: AI benefits take time to materialize. Implementation involves system integration, configuration, and workflow adaptation. A strategic and patient approach is essential for long-term success.

Myth 8: AI Doesn't Need Updates Post-Implementation

Reality: AI technology continuously evolves, necessitating regular updates to maintain effectiveness and compatibility. As a business grows, its AI needs may change, requiring ongoing adjustments.

By dispelling these myths, SMB owners can approach AI automation with clarity and practical expectations. Adopting AI automation can lead to increased efficiency, competitiveness, and innovation, but it must be done thoughtfully and knowledgeably. With these misconceptions addressed, SMBs are better equipped to explore and integrate AI automation into their business practices effectively.

Chapter 3:

Identifying Automation Opportunities in Your Business

Embarking on the AI automation journey as a small or medium-sized business (SMB) demands a deliberate approach to identifying where automation can make a meaningful difference. This chapter provides a roadmap to discovering these opportunities by highlighting signs that a process is ripe for automation, advising on how to prioritize for maximum impact, and guiding you through business process mapping for an effective automation strategy. By the end, you'll be well-prepared to pinpoint automation potentials that can refine operations, boost efficiency, and cultivate a robust and adaptable business environment.

Signs a Process is Ripe for Automation

High Repetitiveness and Volume

Processes that are performed frequently and are time-intensive are prime candidates for AI automation. Automating such tasks liberates your team to focus on more complex, value-adding activities.

Prone to Human Error

Tasks that require meticulous attention and are error-prone, like financial reconciliations or data validation, can gain immensely from AI's precision, thus improving your operational quality.

Time-Sensitive and Critical for Operations

Automating processes that are essential for operational fluency or customer satisfaction, such as real-time inventory updates, can prevent delays and maintain business continuity.

Involves Multiple Systems and Datasets

Automation can effectively synchronize data across various systems, streamlining processes that would be inefficient if done manually.

High Labor Costs

When a process consumes considerable manpower, automation can reallocate resources more strategically, optimizing labor costs and enhancing job satisfaction by eliminating monotonous work.

Scalability Issues

As your business expands, automation ensures that processes can handle increased loads efficiently, crucial for businesses experiencing growth spurts or seasonal peaks.

Consistency and Standardization Required

For processes demanding uniformity, AI systems can ensure adherence to standards, crucial in areas like compliance reporting and quality assurance.

Employee Feedback

Your team can offer insights into processes that are cumbersome or inefficient. Their firsthand experience is a valuable source for identifying automation opportunities.

Chapter 4:

Mapping Your Business Processes for AI Automation

As you set out on your AI automation adventure, it is essential to grasp the complexities of your organization's processes. Business process mapping is a foundational strategy to unearth areas that are ripe for automation.

By recognizing these signs and strategically approaching the integration of AI automation, SMBs can transform potential challenges into opportunities for growth and innovation.

Understanding Business Process Mapping

Business process mapping is akin to charting a course through your organizational operations, depicting the steps, responsibilities, timings, and resources involved. This detailed visual guide provides a macro and micro perspective of your workflows, pinpointing inefficiencies and paving the way for improvements through AI automation.

Map out each process, detailing the steps involved, the employees responsible, the time taken, and the systems used. This mapping will reveal inefficiencies and complexities that automation can resolve, laying the groundwork for a smooth transition to AI-powered operations.

The Benefits of Process Mapping

- **Clarity and Insight:** Mapping gives a transparent view of your workflows, pinpointing inefficiencies that can be streamlined.

- **Communication and Collaboration:** A visual map enhances understanding and cooperation, aligning teams on process flow and roles.

- **Standardization and Consistency:** Process mapping aids in unifying procedures across the business, minimizing errors, and ensuring quality.

- **Foundation for Automation:** It highlights manual, repetitive steps that are ideal for AI automation.

Steps to Effective Business Process Mapping

1. **Identify the Processes:** List key processes critical to your operations, focusing on those integral to your product/service delivery, customer satisfaction, or resource-heavy.

2. **Gather the Right Team:** Form a team with in-depth knowledge of the workflow, including process participants and managers, for valuable insights.

3. **Define the Scope:** Clearly establish the boundaries of the process mapping to maintain focus and avoid overextending the scope.

4. **Collect Data:** Compile information on the steps, sequence, roles, and resources involved in the process.

5. **Choose Your Mapping Tool:** Select an appropriate tool for documenting the process map, from simple pen and paper to advanced software, based on your needs and process complexity.

6. **Map the Process:** Document each step from start to finish, capturing every action, decision point, and transition.

7. **Validate and Refine:** Collaborate with your team and stakeholders to ensure the map's accuracy and make necessary refinements.

8. **Identify Automation** Opportunities: Spot steps that are rule-based, repetitive, and time-intensive - these are prime for AI automation.

9. **Prioritize:** Evaluate automation opportunities based on potential benefits such as cost savings, time

efficiency, error reduction, and impact on customer satisfaction.

By meticulously mapping out your business processes, you create a blueprint that reveals where AI automation can be most effective. This systematic approach ensures that you're not just automating for the sake of technology but are making strategic decisions that align with your business objectives.

With a comprehensive map and a clear understanding of where AI can be integrated, your organization is well-positioned to harness the power of automation for enhanced efficiency, growth, and competitiveness.

Chapter 5:

Moving Forward with Automation

Having meticulously mapped your business processes and pinpointed automation opportunities, you stand on the threshold of AI automation. This chapter is dedicated to the next phase—strategically deploying automation to address critical needs and maximize return on investment (ROI).

Prioritizing Processes for Automation

Effective prioritization isn't just about the order of task automation—it's about grasping each process's strategic value to your business. Prioritization ensures that your automation initiatives yield tangible benefits, secure stakeholder buy-in, efficiently allocate resources, and facilitate quick wins that propel your automation journey forward.

Criteria for Prioritizing Processes

1. **Impact on Business Objectives:** Prioritize processes that are key to meeting strategic goals.//
2. **Return on Investment (ROI):** Focus on processes with high potential for cost savings and revenue generation.

3. **Time Savings:** Target time-intensive, manual tasks that can significantly improve productivity and job satisfaction.

4. **Error Reduction:** Automate error-prone processes to increase accuracy and reduce risk.

5. **Scalability: Consider processes** that, when automated, enable your business to scale effectively.

6. **Customer Impact:** Give precedence to processes that directly enhance customer satisfaction and service quality.

Steps to Prioritize Processes for Automation

1. **List and Score:** Rate each automation opportunity based on impact, ROI, time savings, error reduction, scalability, and customer impact.

2. **Analyze Dependencies:** Understand interdependencies between processes to ensure logical sequencing in automation.

3. **Assess Feasibility:** Balance the ambition of automation against practicality, considering technical and resource constraints.

4. **Create a Roadmap:** Develop a phased plan, beginning with high-value, feasible processes and progressing to more complex automation projects.

5. **Engage Stakeholders:** Involve key stakeholders in the planning process for additional insights and to refine your approach.

6. **Review and Adapt:** Maintain flexibility in your automation strategy, adjusting as necessary in response to business changes, technological progress, or outcomes from initial projects.

Implementing the Automation Roadmap

Once you've prioritized processes, it's time to start actual automation. Implementing your automation roadmap involves:

1. **Selecting AI Tools and Technologies:** Choose tools that align with the specific processes identified in your map.

2. **Developing Implementation Plans:** For each process, create detailed implementation plans, including timelines, resources, and milestones.

3. **Executing Automation Projects:** Methodically roll out automation projects, adhering to the established plans and timelines.

4. **Monitoring and Measuring Impact:** Continuously monitor the effects of automation on business processes, adjusting as needed to optimize performance.

5. **Scaling Automation Efforts:** As initial projects succeed, scale your automation efforts to encompass more processes, reinforcing the cycle of improvement and growth.

By investing time in process mapping and prioritization, you establish a solid foundation for AI automation. This strategic approach ensures that automation drives efficiency, accuracy, and responsiveness, transforming your business into a model of agility and innovation in the marketplace.

Remember, successful automation is not just about technology; it's about enhancing your business's operations and competitive edge in an ever-changing economic landscape. With a clear roadmap and a focus on strategic value, your journey towards AI automation is well underway.

Quick Wins vs. Long-Term Investments

As businesses venture into AI automation, they are faced with a strategic decision: to chase quick wins that offer immediate gratification or to engage in long-term investments that hold the promise of ongoing growth and transformation. This chapter delves into the art of striking a balance between these two approaches, ensuring that your automation strategy not only captures early successes but also lays the groundwork for lasting value.

Understanding Quick Wins

Quick wins are automation projects that can be rapidly implemented, yielding benefits in the short term. These projects are generally characterized by low complexity and high impact, offering a swift ROI and momentum for broader automation initiatives.

Characteristics of Quick Wins:

6. **Low Complexity:** Easy to automate processes.

- **High Impact:** They significantly improve key areas such as efficiency, error rate, or customer experience.

- **Short Implementation** Time: Deployment is quick, typically ranging from weeks to a few months.

- **Minimal Risk:** With clear outcomes and low investment, the financial and operational risks are reduced.

Benefits of Pursuing Quick Wins:

- **Demonstrate Value:** They serve as proof of concept, showcasing the potential of AI automation.

- **Gain Buy-in: Successes** help to secure support from various stakeholders.

- **Build Experience:** They offer a chance to learn about AI technology and processes.

Understanding Long-Term Investments

Long-term investments are more intricate initiatives that call for substantial time, resources, and strategic planning. Their goal is to drive transformative changes within the business, yielding benefits that accrue over time.

Characteristics of Long-Term Investments:

- **High Complexity:** Automation of complex processes or system integrations.

- **Strategic Impact:** Potential to revolutionize business operations and create new growth avenues.

- **Extended Implementation:** Timelines span several months to years.

- **Higher Risk and Investment:** Requires greater resources and carries **more** significant risks.

Benefits of Long-Term Investments:

- Sustainable Growth: They can significantly enhance business efficiency and scalability.
- Competitive Differentiation: Using AI as a means of innovation can set your business apart.
- Deep Transformation: Potential to profoundly alter your business model and market position.

Balancing Quick Wins and Long-Term Investments

To strike a strategic balance in your AI automation endeavors, consider these steps:

- Assess Your Business Needs: Gauge both immediate and long-term objectives to inform your strategy.
- Evaluate Your Resources: Look at your budget, expertise, and tech infrastructure to determine what's feasible.
- Prioritize Based on Impact: Choose projects by their potential impact, considering the scale and timing of benefits.
- Develop a Roadmap: Craft a plan that includes both quick wins and long-term investments, tailored to your business's priorities and change capacity.
- Implement, Measure, and Adapt: Execute your projects while monitoring progress and outcomes, ready to refine your strategy based on early learnings.
- Communicate and Celebrate Successes: Share results and milestones to reinforce the value of your automation efforts.
- Leverage Quick Wins to Fuel Long-Term Projects: Use the success and credibility from quick wins as a springboard for tackling more ambitious projects.

By discerning the optimal balance between quick wins and long-term investments in AI automation, you can maintain momentum while securing enduring advantages for your business. Quick wins can offer immediate value and foster confidence in AI initiatives, whereas long-term investments can drive substantial, lasting improvements. A thoughtful evaluation of your needs, resources, and ambitions enables you to craft an automation strategy that delivers not only immediate benefits but also a solid foundation for a more efficient and competitive business future.

Chapter 6:

Tools and Techniques for Process Identification

To harness the transformative power of AI automation effectively, pinpointing the right processes for automation is essential.

The overarching goal in the identification process is to recognize operations that significantly benefit from automation—those that are manual, repetitive, and error-prone, yet vital to your business's success or customer satisfaction.

Workflow Analysis:

Description: An in-depth review of workflows to spot inefficiencies or redundancies.

Application: Map each step of a process to locate delays or complications.

Benefit: Identifies specific process stages that are prime for automation.

Employee Surveys and Interviews:

Description: Insights from your workforce can reveal which processes are inefficient or burdensome.

Application: Use surveys and interviews to collect employee feedback on task inefficiencies.

Benefit: Captures firsthand insights, aligning automation with real needs.

Data Analysis:

Description: Using data to identify patterns or anomalies indicating inefficiencies.

Application: Analyze metrics or error rates to find underperforming processes.

Benefit: Offers a data-centric method to target automation opportunities objectively.

Benchmarking:

Description: Assessing your processes against industry standards or competitors.

Application: Identify where your business falls short compared to peers.

Benefit: Aligns automation with competitive and industry benchmarks.

Customer Feedback:

Description: Utilizing customer opinions to pinpoint service issues.

Application: Analyze service inquiries and reviews for common customer complaints.

Benefit: Directs automation efforts towards enhancing customer satisfaction.

Technology Scouting:

Description: Keeping abreast with the latest AI and automation technologies.

Application: Evaluate new tools for their applicability to your business.

Benefit: Positions your business at the forefront of technology, enabling proactive automation.

Pilot Testing:

Description: Conducting small-scale tests to gauge automation's impact.

Application: Trial a low-risk process for automation, monitor outcomes and feedback.

Benefit: Provides a safe environment to test and refine automation before large-scale deployment.

Implementing Your Findings

After identifying automation candidates using these methodologies, you must prioritize them and develop a strategic implementation plan. This plan should factor in potential ROI, impact on stakeholders, and congruence with business objectives.

Identifying the optimal processes for AI automation blends analytical prowess with business intuition. By employing the tools and techniques detailed in this chapter, you can ground your AI automation initiatives in strategic insight, ensuring they drive meaningful and enduring enhancements throughout your organization.

The aim is not merely to automate for automation's sake but to innovate, reshaping your processes in ways that fuel significant and sustainable progress.

Chapter 7:

Planning Your AI Automation Strategy

Diving into AI automation is an exciting move that can boost your business's productivity, lower expenses, and encourage fresh, creative ideas. But to truly reap these rewards, it's important to have a solid plan that matches up with your company's goals, builds on what you do best, and tackles the unique hurdles you face.

In this part of the book, we'll cover the essential steps to build a strong AI automation plan. We'll look at setting specific goals, gauging how ready your business is to adopt new tech, and picking the best technologies and partners for your needs.

We'll also talk about why it's crucial to get everyone on board, manage changes well, and keep learning, to make sure your AI automation efforts are supported and can keep up with your business as it grows and changes.

Setting Clear Objectives for Automation

Embarking on AI automation without clear goals is akin to sailing blind. You may progress, but without a true course or endpoint. Setting specific, quantifiable, and attainable goals is vital to steer your automation endeavors, offering numerous benefits:

- **Direction**: They provide a clear direction for your automation efforts, ensuring all activities contribute toward a common goal.

- **Alignment**: They help align automation projects with your business's strategic priorities, ensuring resources are invested wisely.

- **Measurement**: Clear objectives enable you to measure progress and success, facilitating informed decision-making and continuous improvement.

- **Motivation**: They inspire and motivate your team, offering a clear vision of what you aim to achieve and why it matters.

Steps to Setting Clear Objectives

1. **Assess Your Business Needs**:
    - Begin by thoroughly assessing your business's current challenges, opportunities, and strategic goals. Identify areas where automation can have the most significant impact, such as improving efficiency, reducing costs, or enhancing customer satisfaction.
    - Engage with stakeholders across your organization to gather insights and

perspectives on potential automation opportunities and priorities.

2. **Define Specific Goals**:
   - Based on your assessment, define specific, actionable goals for your AI automation initiatives. These goals should be closely tied to your business's strategic objectives and address key challenges or opportunities identified.
   - Ensure your goals are SMART: Specific, Measurable, Achievable, Relevant, and Timebound. For example, rather than setting a vague goal like "improve customer service," aim for something more precise, such as "reduce response time for customer inquiries by 50% within six months through automation."

3. **Prioritize Your Objectives**:
   - Given limited resources and the potential complexity of AI automation projects, it's essential to prioritize your objectives. Consider factors such as potential impact, feasibility, and alignment with strategic priorities to determine which goals should be addressed first.
   - Develop a prioritization matrix or use a scoring system to objectively assess and rank your

objectives, ensuring consensus among stakeholders.

4. **Break Down Objectives into Actionable Step**s:

    - Once you have your prioritized list of objectives, break them down into smaller, actionable steps. This approach helps translate high-level goals into specific tasks and milestones, making them more manageable and achievable.

    - For each objective, identify the key actions required, assign responsibilities, and establish timelines. This detailed planning helps ensure clarity of execution and accountability.

5. **Communicate and Align**:

    - Clearly communicate your automation objectives and the rationale behind them to all relevant stakeholders, including your team, management, and any external partners. Ensuring everyone understands and is aligned with these goals is crucial for successful implementation.

    - Encourage feedback and be prepared to refine your objectives based on new insights or changing circumstances.

6. **Monitor and Adapt**:

- Establish a process for regularly monitoring progress toward your objectives, using predefined metrics and milestones. This monitoring enables you to track achievements, identify challenges, and measure the impact of your automation efforts.

- Be prepared to adapt your objectives and strategy based on performance data, feedback, and evolving business needs. Flexibility is key to responding effectively to challenges and seizing new opportunities as they arise.

Setting clear objectives is a vital first step in planning your AI automation strategy, providing a roadmap for focused and effective implementation.

Also remember that these objectives are not set in stone; they should evolve with your business, reflecting new insights, priorities, and market conditions.

Understanding Your Automation Readiness

Before diving headfirst into the world of AI automation, it's crucial to gauge your business's readiness for such a transformative journey. Understanding your automation readiness not only sets the stage for a successful implementation but also helps identify potential gaps or areas that need strengthening to fully leverage AI capabilities.

Assessing Your Technological Infrastructure

The foundation of any successful AI automation initiative is robust technological infrastructure. Evaluate your current IT systems, software, and hardware to determine if they can support advanced AI applications. Consider factors like data storage capacity, processing power, network stability, and security protocols. If your infrastructure is outdated or lacks the necessary capabilities, identifying these shortcomings early allows you to plan for necessary upgrades or adjustments.

Evaluating Organizational Culture and Mindset

AI automation isn't just about technology, but people. The success of your automation efforts will largely depend on your team's willingness and ability to adapt to new ways of working. Assess your organizational culture to determine if there's a mindset of innovation and openness to change. Encourage a culture where automation is viewed as a tool for empowerment, not a threat, fostering an environment where employees are eager to embrace new technologies and contribute to their successful deployment.

Understanding Process Maturity

The effectiveness of AI automation is significantly influenced by the maturity of your existing processes. Analyze your business processes to identify which ones are standardized, documented, and stable. For example, the processes that are erratic, poorly defined, or frequently changing are less suitable for immediate automation and may require optimization before they can be effectively automated.

This understanding will help you prioritize which processes to automate first and which to refine.

Gauging Data Readiness

AI systems thrive on data. The quality, quantity, and accessibility of your data are critical factors in the success of AI automation. Assess your data management practices to ensure that data is accurate, consistent, and readily available. If your data is siloed, incomplete, or of poor quality, you'll need to address these issues before proceeding with automation, as they can significantly impact the effectiveness and reliability of AI applications.

Identifying Skills and Knowledge Gaps

Implementing AI automation requires specific skills and knowledge, both in terms of developing and managing AI solutions and in terms of the broader workforce adapting to new automated processes. Identify any skills gaps within your organization that could hinder your automation efforts. This may involve upskilling current employees, hiring new talent with the necessary expertise, or partnering with external vendors or consultants.

Developing a Supportive Leadership and Governance Structure

Strong leadership and governance are essential for steering AI automation initiatives in the right direction and ensuring they align with broader business objectives. Evaluate whether your leadership team understands and supports AI automation and whether you have the governance structures in place to manage these initiatives effectively. This includes establishing clear roles, responsibilities, and decision-making processes related to AI automation.

Understanding your automation readiness is a critical step in planning your AI automation strategy. It provides a realistic assessment of where your business stands, what needs to be addressed, and how best to proceed with your automation initiatives.

By taking the time to evaluate your readiness across these key dimensions, you can set the stage for a successful transformation that leverages AI automation to drive efficiency, innovation, and competitive advantage.

Building an Automation Roadmap

With a thorough understanding of your automation readiness, you can develop a more informed and effective implementation roadmap.

This roadmap acts as a strategic plan, outlining the steps your business will take to implement AI automation effectively, ensuring that each phase aligns with your overarching business goals and objectives. It will help you:

- **Prioritize Initiatives:** Clearly define which processes will be automated and in what order, based on their potential impact and your business's readiness.

- **Allocate Resources:** Identify the resources required for each phase of automation, including budget, personnel, and technology.

- **Manage Change:** Outline the steps needed to manage the organizational change that accompanies automation, ensuring smooth transitions and widespread adoption.

- **Measure Success:** Establish metrics and milestones to track the progress and impact of your automation initiatives.

Steps to Building Your Automation Roadmap

1. **Set Clear Objectives**:
    - Begin by revisiting the objectives you set for your AI automation initiatives. These objectives should be specific, measurable, achievable, relevant, and timebound (SMART).

- Ensure that each objective aligns with your broader business goals, providing a clear rationale for why you're pursuing automation.

2. **Assess Your Current State**:

- Evaluate your current processes, technology infrastructure, and organizational readiness, as discussed in the previous sections.
- Identify any gaps or areas that need improvement to support your automation goals.

3. **Prioritize Processes for Automation**:

- Based on your assessment, prioritize the processes that are most suited for automation, considering factors like potential impact, readiness, and strategic importance.
- Develop a phased approach, starting with quick wins that can deliver immediate benefits and build momentum for more complex initiatives.

4. **Define Resources and Responsibilities:**

- For each automation initiative, clearly define the resources required, including technology, personnel, and budget.
- Assign responsibilities, ensuring that there are clear owners for each phase of the roadmap, from initial development to ongoing management.

5. **Develop an Implementation Schedule:**
   - Create a detailed schedule for your automation initiatives, outlining key milestones and timelines.
   - Ensure that the schedule is realistic, allowing sufficient time for development, testing, and deployment, as well as for addressing any unforeseen challenges.

6. **Plan for Change Management:**
   - Anticipate the organizational changes that automation will bring, and develop strategies to manage these changes effectively.
   - Include plans for communication, training, and support, ensuring that employees are prepared for and engaged with the automation initiatives.

7. **Establish Metrics for Success:**
   - Define how you will measure the success of your automation initiatives, identifying key performance indicators (KPIs) that align with your objectives.
   - Plan for regular reviews of these metrics, allowing you to track progress, assess the impact, and make adjustments as needed.

8. **Communicate and Collaborate:**

- Share your automation roadmap with key stakeholders across the organization, soliciting their input and ensuring their buyin.

- Foster a collaborative environment where feedback is encouraged, and different departments can contribute to the success of the automation initiatives.

Building an automation roadmap is a critical step in your AI automation strategy, providing a clear and actionable plan for how your business will leverage AI to achieve its goals.

With this roadmap in hand, you're well-equipped to embark on a successful AI automation journey, transforming your business processes, enhancing efficiency, and driving innovation.

Key Considerations: Budget, Timeline, and Resources

These three elements are the bedrock of your planning process, ensuring that your automation initiatives are feasible, sustainable, and aligned with your business objectives.

Let's clarify each of these key considerations to understand how to effectively integrate them into your AI automation strategy.

Budget: Balancing Cost and Value

The financial investment in AI automation can vary widely, depending on the scope and complexity of your projects. Take the following steps to ensure your automation initiatives deliver value without straining your financial resources.

1. **Cost Assessment:**
   - Begin by estimating the costs associated with each phase of your automation projects, including software acquisition, system integration, training, and ongoing maintenance.
   - Consider potential cost savings and efficiency gains that automation can bring, helping to offset initial expenses and provide long-term value.

2. **Funding and Approval:**
   - Secure the necessary funding and approvals for your budget, presenting a clear business case that outlines the expected ROI from your automation initiatives.
   - Be transparent about potential risks and how they will be mitigated to ensure stakeholder confidence and support.

3. **Cost Monitoring:**

- Establish a system for monitoring and controlling your automation budget, ensuring that expenses align with planned projections and adjusting as necessary.

- Regularly review the financial performance of your automation projects, assessing their impact on your business's bottom line.

Timeline: Setting Realistic Expectations

A realistic and well-structured timeline is essential for coordinating the various elements of your automation strategy and ensuring timely progress.

1. **Phased Approach:**

    - Adopt a phased approach to implementation, starting with pilot projects or quick wins that can deliver early results and inform broader initiatives.

    - Allow sufficient time for each phase, including planning, development, testing, deployment, and evaluation.

2. **Flexibility:**

    - While it's important to adhere to your timeline, remain flexible and adaptable to unforeseen challenges or opportunities that may arise.

- Build in buffer periods to accommodate delays or unexpected issues, ensuring that they don't derail your overall strategy.

3. **Milestone Tracking:**

- Define clear milestones and checkpoints throughout your timeline, allowing you to track progress, celebrate achievements, and identify areas needing attention.
- Use these milestones to facilitate regular updates with stakeholders, keeping them informed and engaged with your automation journey.

Resources: Leveraging Assets Effectively

The successful implementation of AI automation depends on having the right resources in place, including technology, personnel, and knowledge.

1. **Technology Assessment:**

- Evaluate your existing technology infrastructure to determine if it can support your automation goals or if upgrades are necessary.
- Select automation tools and platforms that align with your business needs, ensuring they are scalable, secure, and integrate well with your existing systems.

2. **Team Involvement:**

- Identify the internal teams and individuals who will play key roles in your automation projects, including IT staff, process owners, and end-users.

- Consider external partners or vendors who can provide expertise, technology, or support that complements your internal capabilities.

3. **Knowledge and Training:**

- Assess the training needs of your team, ensuring they have the skills and knowledge to implement and manage AI automation effectively.

- Foster a culture of continuous learning, encouraging employees to stay informed about AI trends, best practices, and emerging technologies.

Incorporating budget, timeline, and resources into your AI automation strategy is about creating a framework that ensures your initiatives are practical, impactful, and sustainable.

By carefully considering these key factors, you can develop a strategy that is well-resourced, financially viable, and aligned with your business's goals and timelines.

With this solid foundation, your AI automation journey is poised for success, ready to enhance your business processes, drive efficiency, and foster innovation.

Chapter 8:

Outsourcing Your AI Automation Projects

As you continue on the AI automation journey, outsourcing can be a strategic move, offering benefits like specialized expertise and cost efficiencies, enhancing your automation capabilities.

However, it also poses challenges, such as vendor selection, communication, seamless integration with your current processes, and retaining control over project quality and outcomes.

We'll address them in subchapters to follow.

The Benefits of Outsourcing AI Automation

AI automation presents unparalleled opportunities for business enhancement, but not all companies can develop in-house capabilities. Outsourcing offers several benefits:

- **Access to Specialized Expertise:** Outsourcing gives you immediate access to experts in AI automation, equipped with the latest knowledge and experience.

- **Cost Efficiency:** It can be more cost-effective than building an in-house team, with a variable cost structure and no need for significant capital investment in technology.

- **Focus on Core Business Activities:** Outsourcing allows your internal team to concentrate on strategic business functions while experts handle the technical aspects.

- **Scalability and Flexibility:** Outsourcing provides the adaptability to scale efforts based on evolving business needs and offers a diverse skill set that can be tailored to different projects.

- **Risk Mitigation:** Established outsourcing firms bring a proven track record and adhere to best practices, helping to reduce the risk of project failure and ensuring compliance and security.

Outsourcing AI automation can strategically position you for growth, providing expertise, efficiency, and focus while mitigating risks. It's essential to select the right partner and foster a collaborative relationship that supports your business goals for successful AI automation endeavors.

How to Find and Select the Right Vendor or Agency

The success of AI automation projects largely depends on the chosen vendor or agency. Here's how to find and select the right partner:

- **Understand Your Needs and Goals:** Define your project scope and establish clear objectives, including measurable goals and KPIs.

- **Research Potential Vendors:** Seek vendors with a solid industry reputation, expertise in AI automation, and technological proficiency.

- **Evaluate Their Experience:** Assess their track record in similar projects, review their portfolio, and ensure they are well-versed with modern AI tools and technologies.

Outsourcing AI automation requires a strategic approach to reap the full benefits. By carefully selecting a vendor that aligns with your business needs and fostering a collaborative relationship, you can leverage the advantages of outsourcing to achieve your automation goals and drive business success.

Evaluating Vendor Capabilities

Once you have a shortlist of potential vendors, delve deeper to evaluate their capabilities and how well they align with your project requirements.

- **Consultation and Proposal:** Engage with the vendors to discuss your project in detail. A reputable vendor should offer insightful consultations and propose tailored solutions that address your specific needs.

- **References and Reviews:** Request references from past clients and check online reviews to gauge their reliability, responsiveness, and the quality of their work.

- **Cultural Fit:** Consider the vendor's corporate culture and values. Ensuring a good cultural fit can enhance collaboration and communication throughout the project.

Assessing Cost and Value

While cost is an important consideration, it's crucial to balance it with the value the vendor brings to your project.

- **Transparent Pricing:** Look for vendors who provide clear, transparent pricing structures. Understand what is included in their quotes and be wary of hidden costs.

- **Value for Money:** Evaluate the cost relative to the value the vendor offers, considering their expertise, technology, and the potential ROI they can deliver for your project.

Communication and Collaboration

Effective communication and collaboration are key to the success of any outsourced project.

- **Communication Channels:** Ensure the vendor has robust communication channels and processes in place. You should feel confident in their ability to keep you informed and involved throughout the project.

- **Collaboration Approach:** The vendor should view the relationship as a partnership, showing a willingness to collaborate closely with your team, understand your business, and adapt to your feedback.

Making the Selection

With all the information and insights gathered, you can make an informed decision on the right vendor for your AI automation project.

- **Decision Matrix:** Create a decision matrix that evaluates each vendor against your key criteria, such as expertise, experience, cost, and cultural fit.

- **Trial Project:** If possible, consider starting with a small trial project to assess the vendor's capabilities and the working relationship before committing to a larger engagement.

By thoroughly understanding your needs, conducting diligent research, evaluating capabilities, and ensuring effective communication and collaboration, you can establish a successful partnership that drives your business forward with innovative AI automation solutions.

Preparing a Comprehensive Brief for Your Automation Project

When you decide to outsource your AI automation projects, one of the critical steps to ensure the success of your collaboration with a vendor is the preparation of a comprehensive project brief.

A project brief is essentially a blueprint for your AI automation project. It provides your vendor with essential insights and information, enabling them to understand your vision, align their approach with your goals, and deliver solutions that meet your expectations.

A well-prepared brief can significantly enhance the clarity, efficiency, and outcome of your AI automation initiative.

Key Components of a Comprehensive Project Brief

1. **Project Background and Context:**

    - Provide an Overview of your business, including your industry, products or services, and the specific challenges or opportunities you aim to address through AI automation.

    - Explain the motivation behind the project and its significance to your broader business objectives.

2. **Project Objectives:**

   - Clearly define the goals you intend to achieve with your AI automation project. Be specific about the outcomes you expect and how they will be measured.

   - Highlight any key performance indicators (KPIs) or benchmarks that will be used to evaluate the project's success.

3. **Scope and Deliverables:**

   - Outline the specific processes or functions you wish to automate, detailing the expected deliverables and any particular requirements or constraints.

   - Specify any critical milestones or phases within the project, along with their associated timelines.

4. **Target Audience and Stakeholders**:

   - Identify the internal or external stakeholders who will be impacted by or involved in the project, including their roles and interests.

   - Consider any user requirements or preferences that should be considered when designing and implementing an automation solution.

5. **Technical Requirements and Integration:**
    - Detail the technical specifications and requirements of your project, including any existing systems or platforms with which the automation solution must integrate.
    - Address data management considerations, such as data sources, formats, and privacy requirements.

6. **Budget and Resource Constraints:**
    - Provide information on the available budget for the project, highlighting any financial constraints or considerations.
    - Outline the resources, including personnel and technology, that your organization will provide or require for the project.

7. **Communication and Reporting:**
    - Establish preferred channels and communication frequency throughout the project. Specify how updates, feedback, and decisions will be shared.
    - Define the reporting structure and requirements, including the format and content of progress reports.

Tips for Preparing an Effective Project Brief

- **Be Clear and Concise:** Use clear, straightforward language to convey your requirements and expectations. Avoid jargon or ambiguity that could lead to confusion.

- **Collaborate with Key Stakeholders:** Engage with relevant stakeholders within your organization to gather input and ensure that the brief reflects a comprehensive understanding of your needs and goals.

- **Be Open to Dialogue:** Consider the project brief as a starting point for discussion. Be open to questions, feedback, and suggestions from your vendor, as this can lead to a more tailored and effective automation solution.

- **Review and Revise**: Before finalizing the brief, review it thoroughly to ensure all critical information is included and clearly articulated. Be prepared to revise the brief based on input from your vendor or further reflection on your project's needs.

Defining Goals and Expectations

Establishing a mutual understanding begins with a clear articulation of what you aim to achieve with your AI automation project.

- **Project Goals:** Identify and communicate the specific objectives you intend to accomplish. These goals should be SMART: Specific, Measurable, Achievable, Relevant, and Time-bound.

- **Expectations:** Set clear expectations regarding the vendor's role, the level of quality, and the milestones that need to be reached. It's important that these expectations are realistic and agreed upon by both parties.

Outlining Scope of Work and Deliverables

A well-defined scope ensures everyone is on the same page about what needs to be done.

- **Scope of Work:** Detail the work that will be carried out by the vendor. This should include the processes to be automated, the technology stack to be used, and any other pertinent details.

- C**Deliverables:** clearly define what the vendor is expected to deliver, including software, documentation, training materials, and any other outputs.

Agreeing on Budget and Timeline

Financial clarity and scheduling are critical to a smooth project execution.

- **Budget:** Discuss and agree on the project budget. Ensure that the costs are transparent and that both parties understand what is covered within the budget.

- **Timeline:** Establish a realistic timeline for the project, with key milestones and deadlines. It should allow some flexibility to meet any unforeseen challenges.

Collaboration Framework

With these aspects clearly outlined, you can create a robust framework for collaboration.

- **Communication Plan:** Develop a plan that specifies how often you will communicate, through which channels, and who the primary contacts will be.

- **Performance Metrics:** Agree on the metrics that will be used to measure project success. These should link back to the initial goals and be trackable.

- **Risk Management:** Identify potential risks and agree on a strategy for mitigating them. This should include contingency plans for critical parts of the project.

- **Contract and Documentation:** Solidify your understanding with formal contracts and documentation. This ensures that all parties have a reference point for the project's terms and conditions.

Chapter 9:

Working with AI Automation Vendors

Selecting an AI automation provider is the first step in a journey that shapes your project's success.

The quality of your relationship with vendors affects not only your project but also future collaborations and your business's automation progress.

This chapter provides best practices for interactions, emphasizing transparency, trust, and teamwork.

Effective Communication with Providers

Effective communication with AI providers is essential in a complex, fast-moving field. It's the foundation of every successful project.

Communication ensures both parties are on the same page regarding goals, timelines, and outcomes, avoiding misunderstandings and building trust.

Communication Setup

- **Choose Communication Tools:** Agree on the most accessible and convenient communication methods.

- **Regular Updates:** Establish routine meetings for project updates and adjustments.

- **Assign Communication Leads:** Designate team members from both sides to streamline communication.

Communication Improvement

- **Be Clear:** Communicate concisely to prevent errors.

- **Encourage Openness:** Create an atmosphere where exchanging ideas and feedback is encouraged.

- **Document Discussions:** Keep records of important communications for reference.

Communication Challenges

- **Address Issues Quickly:** Resolve communication problems as they occur to prevent escalation.

- **Listen First:** Understand the provider's viewpoint before responding to conflicts.

- **Mediation:** If necessary, use a neutral third party to help resolve persistent issues.

Communication for Project Success

- **Align on Vision:** Confirm that the provider understands and supports your project's vision.

- **Adapt Communication**: Modify communication strategies as the project develops.
- **Celebrate Milestones:** Use communication to acknowledge progress, boosting team morale.

Managing the Project: Milestones, Feedback, and Adjustments

Undertaking an AI automation project requires clear milestones, responsive feedback, and the agility to make adjustments. This section outlines effective project management strategies for AI automation efforts.

Establishing Milestones

- Set specific, achievable goals that provide structure and enable progress tracking.
- Collaborate with vendors to create realistic timelines for each phase.
- Regularly monitor and celebrate milestone achievements to maintain alignment and momentum.

Encouraging Feedback

- Create regular opportunities to share ideas and concerns.
- Offer precise, objective feedback focused on improvement.

- Act on feedback quickly, documenting and communicating any changes to stakeholders.

Adapting to Changes

- Prepare for unexpected changes and be ready to adjust plans.
- Make decisions together with your vendor, considering the project's broader implications.
- Document all changes to maintain clarity and alignment among stakeholders.

Effective project management in AI automation calls for dynamic collaboration. By maintaining open communication, adhering to objectives, and adapting to challenges, you can guide your project to success and drive your business forward.

Evaluating Project Success

After execution, it's vital to evaluate the success of your AI automation project to inform future efforts and strategic decisions.

Evaluation goes beyond task completion; it measures the project's impact on business and ROI.

This process encourages continuous improvement and informs further AI investments.

Evaluation Areas

- Compare outcomes to initial objectives and KPIs.
- Review the quality and performance of automated processes.Assess user adoption and satisfaction.
- Analyze the broader business impact, direct and indirect.
- Extract lessons for future project optimizations.

Strategies for Effective Evaluation

- Collect comprehensive data from various sources.
- Involve stakeholders for a multifaceted perspective.
- Utilize benchmarks for contextual success comparison.
- Document and communicate findings, celebrating achievements and identifying improvement areas.
- Use insights for ongoing project enhancement and future planning.

Evaluating your AI automation project is crucial for understanding its effectiveness and value, guiding informed decisions for future innovation, and promoting continuous advancement in your automation initiatives.

Chapter 10:

Scaling Your AI Automation Efforts

Scaling AI automation is an expansive move from isolated success to widespread organizational improvement. Going beyond merely increasing the number of automation projects to a strategic growth and comprehensive integration, consider the following approach:

Build on Initial Successes

- Analyze early automation projects to understand successes and failures.
- Use these insights to gain stakeholder support and shape your scaling strategy.

Plan for Expansion Strategically

- Align scaling with business goals and assess organizational readiness.
- Identify high-impact areas and create a strategic roadmap for growth.
- Prioritize projects and allocate resources efficiently.

Cross-Departmental Collaboration

- Integrate automation across functions for cohesive improvements.
- Encourage communication between departments to share best practices and drive change.

Continuous Optimization and Learning

- Scaling is ongoing; constantly monitor, optimize, and adapt to new business needs.
- Promote a culture of innovation to stay ahead in AI automation.

Overcoming Challenges in Scaling

- Address technical and change resistance challenges effectively.
- Ensure your efforts are resilient and sustainable.

Scaling AI automation requires building on what works, planning strategically, fostering collaboration, and continuously refining your approach.

Deciding Between In-House AI Team or Outsourcing

As your business grows its AI operations, you face a key decision: form an in-house AI team or keep outsourcing?

This choice will shape your project's success and long-term viability. We'll look at the pros and cons of both options to help you decide in line with your goals and context.

Creating an In-House Team

An in-house AI team offers control and cultural fit, allowing for:

- **Direct Oversight:** You can manage projects closely and align with company objectives.

- **Flexibility:** Your team can quickly adjust to business shifts, important in a changing market.

- **Cultural Cohesion:** The team will share your company's values, boosting dedication and teamwork.

- **Skill Growth:** You nurture AI expertise internally, reducing reliance on outside vendors.

- **The Rise of No-code Tools:** Recently, no-code platforms have become a viable option, challenging the need for costly, specialized agency services. (*See Appendix E for details.*)

Challenges:

- Requires investment in hiring, training, and infrastructure.

- Needs a robust internal support system for AI efforts.

Sticking with Outsourcing

Outsourcing gives you flexibility and access to a wide pool of talent:

- **Specialized Skills:** Quickly tap into a range of experts and stay updated with industry trends.

- **Agility:** Easily scale AI tasks to meet changing needs without the fixed costs of an in-house team.

- **Cost Savings:** Ideal for temporary or specialized projects without long-term resource commitment.

Challenges:

- Must manage vendor relationships and ensure they understand your goals.

- Consider data security and compliance when choosing vendors.

Making Your Choice

The decision between an in-house team and outsourcing must be strategic, considering:

- **Readiness:** Assess if you can support an in-house team with your current resources.

- **Business Goals:** Choose the option that aligns with your overall strategy and operational style.

- **Project Needs:** Look at your AI project's scale, complexity, and timeline to decide the best approach.

Whether you build an in-house team or continue outsourcing, think strategically about your immediate and future needs. By evaluating the advantages and challenges of each choice, you can steer your AI initiatives towards contributing lasting value and advancing your company in the digital age.

Recap of Key Takeaways

Throughout this guide, we've delved into various facets of AI automation, from understanding its fundamentals and identifying processes ripe for automation to selecting the right vendors and scaling your efforts. Here's a brief recap of the essential points we've covered:

1. **Understanding AI Automation:** We began by demystifying AI automation, highlighting its potential to transform businesses by enhancing efficiency, accuracy, and productivity.

2. **Identifying Opportunities:** We explored how to spot processes within your business that are prime candidates for automation, emphasizing the importance of strategic selection to maximize impact.

3. **Choosing Vendors:** Selecting the right vendor is crucial for your project's success. We discussed how to evaluate potential partners based on their experience, expertise, and alignment with your project goals.

4. **Project Management:** Effective communication and collaboration with your vendor are key to managing your AI automation project successfully, ensuring that milestones are met, feedback is incorporated, and adjustments are made as needed.

5. **Scaling Efforts:** Once initial projects are successful, scaling AI automation across your organization can amplify its benefits, driving significant improvements in operational efficiency and business agility.

Encouragement to Begin the AI Automation Journey

If you haven't yet started your AI automation journey, there's no better time than now. The field of AI is evolving rapidly, offering new tools and technologies that can provide a competitive advantage to those who adopt them early. Remember, the journey of AI automation is not just about implementing new technologies; it's about transforming your business processes, enhancing your value proposition, and preparing your organization for the future.

For those who have already embarked on this journey, consider this a call to deepen and expand your efforts.

Reflect on the lessons learned, embrace the opportunities to scale, and stay curious and informed about the latest developments in the field.

Next Steps and Resources for Further Learning

As you move forward, whether you're just starting or looking to expand your AI automation initiatives, here are some steps and resources to guide your continued journey:

- **Educate Yourself** and Your Team: Invest in education and training to build a solid understanding of AI automation within your organization. Online courses, webinars, and industry conferences can provide valuable insights and knowledge.

- **Develop a Strategic Plan:** Based on the insights gained from this guide, develop a strategic plan for implementing or scaling AI automation in your organization. Define clear objectives, identify key processes for automation, and establish a roadmap for execution.

- **Leverage Online Resources:** Numerous online platforms offer in-depth articles, case studies, and tutorials on AI automation. Websites like Medium, Harvard Business Review, and industry-specific publications can be excellent sources of ongoing information.

- **Join Professional Communities:** Engaging with professional communities can provide support, inspiration, and networking opportunities. Consider joining AI and automation-focused groups on LinkedIn, attending industry meetups, or participating in online forums.

- **Consult with Experts:** If you're unsure where to start or how to overcome specific challenges, don't hesitate to seek advice from experts. Consultants and industry professionals can offer tailored guidance and insights to help you navigate your AI automation journey.

AI automation presents an exciting frontier with the potential to significantly impact how businesses operate and compete. By understanding its principles, strategically implementing projects, and staying attuned to emerging trends, you can harness the power of AI automation to drive innovation and success in your organization.

Embrace the journey with enthusiasm, openness to learning, and a commitment to continuous improvement, and you'll be well-equipped to thrive in the era of AI-driven transformation.

* * *

This introduction has aimed to demystify the world of AI automation, providing you with the knowledge, strategies, and tools necessary to embark on your own automation projects, regardless of your technical background.

From understanding the basics of AI automation to exploring advanced tools and platforms, we've covered a broad spectrum of topics designed to empower you to leverage technology to streamline processes, enhance productivity, and foster innovation.

Whether you're a small business owner looking to automate routine tasks, a manager seeking to optimize team workflows, or an entrepreneur aiming to bring a new digital product to market, the insights and resources provided here are intended to guide you on your path to success.

We hope this eBook will serve you as a valuable resource in your automation endeavors, inspiring you to explore new possibilities, tackle challenges with confidence, and achieve your digital transformation goals. The future of automation is bright and full of potential—embrace it with curiosity, creativity, and a commitment to continuous learning and improvement.

Here's to your success in the exciting world of AI automation!

Appendix A:

AI Automation Evaluation Checklist

Finding Automation Opportunities

- **Identify Repetitive Tasks:** Look for tasks that are performed frequently and require little to no human judgment. These are prime candidates for automation.

- **Assess Data-Heavy Processes:** Consider processes that involve managing large volumes of data. AI can help automate data entry, analysis, and reporting.

- **Review Time-Intensive Work:** Identify work that consumes a disproportionate amount of time, thereby limiting your team's productivity.

- **Evaluate Scalability Needs:** Determine if there are processes that need to scale up or down quickly, which is a challenge for human teams but manageable for AI.

- **Check for High Error Rates:** Pinpoint areas prone to human error, where AI can provide more consistent and accurate results.

- **Analyze Customer Interactions:** Look at customer service operations to see if there are repetitive queries that can be handled by AI-driven chatbots.

- **Consider Decision Support Needs:** Identify decision-making processes that can benefit from AI's predictive analytics and data-driven insights.

- **Map Out Regulatory Compliance:** For industries with stringent compliance requirements, AI can help maintain and monitor compliance through automation.

- **Examine IT Operations:** In IT, tasks like network monitoring, helpdesk operations, and routine maintenance can often be automated.

Preparing for Implementation

- **Prioritize by Impact:** After identifying potential areas for automation, prioritize them based on the potential impact on efficiency, cost savings, and strategic value.

- **Consult Stakeholders:** Engage with team members who are directly involved in the processes to gain their insights and ensure buy-in for the automation project.

- **Estimate Cost-Benefit:** Perform a cost-benefit analysis to understand the financial implications and ROI of implementing AI automation.

- **Develop a Pilot Program:** Start with a small-scale pilot to test the effectiveness of AI automation in a controlled environment before full-scale implementation.

- **Implementation Plan:** Ensure that the AI automation tools you consider can integrate seamlessly with your existing systems and workflows.

- **Assess Skill Gaps:** Determine if your team has the necessary skills to work with AI tools or if training and hiring will be required.

- **Create a Change Management Strategy:** Automation can lead to significant changes in job roles and responsibilities. Prepare a strategy to manage this transition.

- **Create Monitoring and Iteration Plan:** Once implemented, you'll want to continuously monitor the performance of AI automation and make iterative improvements based on feedback and results.

Appendix B:

Project Brief Template

Project Overview

1. **Project Title:** Provide a concise and descriptive title for your automation project.

2. **Project Sponsor:** Identify the executive or senior leader within your organization who is championing this project.

3. **Project Manager:** Overseeing the project's execution, and the primary point of contact.

4. **Project Team:** List the key members of the project team, both internal staff and external partners, along with their roles and responsibilities.

5. **Executive Summary:** Offer a brief Overview of the project, including its purpose, expected benefits, and strategic significance to the organization.

Project Objectives

1. **Primary Objectives:** Clearly define the main goals of the project, ensuring they are specific, measurable, achievable, relevant, and timebound (SMART).

2. **Secondary Objectives:** Outline any additional goals, providing a holistic view of its intended outcomes.

Scope of Work

1. **Processes to be Automated:** Detail the specific processes or tasks that the project will automate, including any relevant subprocesses or components.

2. **Project Boundaries:** Define what is included and excluded from the project scope, clarifying any limitations or constraints.

3. **Deliverables:** List the expected outputs of the project, including software, documentation, training materials, and any other tangible products.

Project Plan

1. **Timeline:** Provide an estimated timeline for the project, including key milestones, phase completions, and review points.

2. **Resources:** Outline the resources required for the project, including technology, personnel, and budget.

3. **Risk Management:** Identify potential risks associated with the project and outline strategies for mitigating these risks.

4. **Change Management:** Describe the approach for managing changes to the project scope, timeline, or deliverables, ensuring flexibility and adaptability.

Communication Plan

1. **Communication Strategy:** Define how project updates, decisions, and feedback will be communicated among team members, stakeholders, and vendors.

2. **Meeting Schedule:** Establish a regular meeting schedule to review progress, address issues, and coordinate activities.

3. **Reporting:** Detail the reporting structure and format for project updates, ensuring transparency and accountability.

Evaluation and Success Criteria

1. **Success Metrics:** Identify the key performance indicators (KPIs) and metrics that will be used to evaluate the project's success, aligning them with the project objectives.

2. **Evaluation Plan:** Outline the process for assessing the project's outcomes, including data collection methods, analysis techniques, and review intervals.

3. **PostImplementation Review:** Plan for a comprehensive review after the project's completion to assess its impact, capture lessons learned, and inform future automation initiatives.

Appendix C:

Tools and Platforms for Process Mapping and Automation

Selecting tools and platforms for process mapping and automation is a vital part of any AI automation initiative. Here are some, along with considerations for making the best choice:

Process Mapping Tools

- **Lucidchart:** Versatile diagramming with real-time collaboration.
- **Microsoft Visio:** Widely-used with integration into Microsoft Office suite.
- **Bizagi Modeler:** User-friendly with drag-and-drop features for process modeling.
- **MindMeister:** Online mind mapping with collaborative features.

Automation Platforms

- **UiPath:** Comprehensive RPA tool suite with a user-friendly interface and strong community support.
- **Automation Anywhere:** Focuses on ease of use, cognitive automation, and cloud-native deployment.
-

- **Blue Prism:** Enterprise-grade RPA for complex processes with strong governance and compliance.
- **Zapier:** Connects apps and services for easy task automation without deep technical expertise.
- **Microsoft Power Automate:** Wide range of automation capabilities with AI-driven insights and Microsoft integration.

Choosing the Right Tools

- **Ease of Use:** The tool should be user-friendly and match your team's capabilities.
- **Scalability:** Ensure the platform can handle your business growth and process complexity.
- **Integration Capabilities:** It should integrate well with current systems and software.
- **Community and Support:** Access to support, forums, and documentation is essential.
- **Cost:** The pricing should be within your budget and provide the necessary features.

By considering these factors and exploring the tools and platforms available, you can make an informed decision that supports your strategic objectives and enhances your operational efficiency.

NOTE that this list is in no way complete, as the new tools emerge almost daily. We encourage you to do your own research.

Appendix D:

Software Tools and Platforms for Automation

Here are some recommended tools and platforms, along with their primary uses and advantages. NOTE that this list is in no way complete, as the new tools emerge almost daily. We encourage you to do your own research.

Task Automation Tools

- **Zapier**
    - User-friendly with a wide array of app integrations.
    - Ideal for routine tasks and favored by non-technical users.
- **IFTTT (If This Then That)**
    - Simple conditional automation with various web services and devices.
    - Great for personal productivity and straightforward business processes.

Robotic Process Automation (RPA) Platforms

- **UiPath**
    - Comprehensive RPA capabilities with an easy-to-use interface.

- Suitable for enterprises looking to automate across multiple applications.
- **Automation Anywhere**
  - Blends RPA with cognitive technologies like NLP and ML.
  - Accessible with cloud deployment, it supports a broad range of automation tasks.
- **Blue Prism**
  - Enterprise-focused, emphasizing security and governance.
  - Ideal for complex integrations and meeting compliance requirements.

Workflow Automation Platforms

- **Microsoft Power Automate**
  - Versatile with deep integration with Microsoft 365.
  - AI builders and pre-built connectors make it powerful for streamlining processes.
- **Nintex**
  - Comprehensive suite for workflow automation and process mapping.
  - Drag-and-drop interface and advanced features cater to various automation levels.

AI-Driven Automation Platforms

- **IBM Watson**

- AI-powered tools for data analysis, NLP, and ML.
- Suitable for businesses seeking intelligent automation solutions.
- **Google Cloud AI**
  - Offers machine learning and AI services with user-friendly APIs.
  - Scalable infrastructure for infusing automation with advanced AI capabilities.

Selecting the Right Tools

To ensure you choose the most appropriate tools for your automation journey, consider the following:

- **Specific Needs**: Match the tool's capabilities with the specific processes you want to automate.
- **Integration:** Ensure the tool can integrate smoothly with your existing systems.
- **Scalability:** Select software that can grow and adapt to your business's evolving needs.
- **User Experience:** Opt for platforms that are user-friendly and align with your team's expertise.
- **Support and Community:** Look for tools with strong support and an active user community.
- **Cost-Effectiveness:** Weigh the tool's features against its cost to ensure a good ROI.

Appendix E:

Bootstrapping Automation with AI and No-code Tools

In the rapidly evolving digital landscape, the democratization of technology has paved the way for businesses of all sizes to leverage AI and automation without the need for extensive resources or technical expertise. This chapter delves into the world of bootstrapping automation, focusing on how AI and no-code tools can provide a rapid, cost-effective solution for automating processes and developing simple software applications like chatbots and custom dashboards.

Introduction

In an era where technology evolves at breakneck speed, the ability to quickly adapt and innovate is not just an advantage; it's a necessity for businesses of all sizes. Enter the world of bootstrapping automation—a realm where AI and no-code tools democratize technology, making powerful automation accessible to everyone, regardless of their technical expertise or financial resources.

This approach is particularly appealing for small to medium-sized enterprises (SMEs) that may not have the luxury of large IT departments or substantial technology budgets. But it's not just for smaller players; even larger organizations can benefit from the agility and innovation that bootstrapping automation facilitates.

The Rise of no-code Platforms

At the heart of bootstrapping automation are no-code platforms, revolutionary tools that enable users to create applications, automate workflows, and analyze data—all without writing a single line of code. These platforms come with intuitive interfaces, drag-and-drop functionalities, and a plethora of prebuilt templates and integrations, making them accessible to users of all skill levels.

no-code platforms are not just about ease of use; they're about empowerment. They empower business users, analysts, and nontechnical staff to bring their ideas to life, automate tedious tasks, and contribute directly to their organization's digital transformation efforts.

The Role of AI in Bootstrapping Automation

AI amplifies the power of no-code platforms, adding layers of intelligence and adaptability to automated processes. AI can analyze vast amounts of data to identify patterns, predict outcomes, and make decisions, transforming routine automation into dynamic, intelligent workflows.

In the context of bootstrapping automation, AI tools integrated into no-code platforms can help businesses automate complex processes that would otherwise require sophisticated programming skills or deep data science expertise. From chatbots that handle customer inquiries to predictive models that inform business decisions, AI is making advanced technology more accessible and impactful.

Why Bootstrap Automation?

- Cost Efficiency: Bootstrapping automation allows businesses to implement powerful solutions without significant upfront investment, reducing financial barriers to innovation and efficiency.

- Speed and Agility: In today's fast-paced business environment, the ability to quickly adapt and respond to changes can be a gamechanger. no-code platforms enable rapid development and deployment, helping businesses stay agile and competitive.

- Empowerment and Collaboration: By enabling nontechnical users to participate in automation and application development, no-code platforms foster a more collaborative, innovative culture within organizations. They break down silos between IT and business units, encouraging cross-functional teams to work together towards common goals.

- Focus on Core Business: By automating routine tasks and processes, businesses can free up valuable time and resources to focus on strategic initiatives and core activities that drive growth and value.

Bootstrapping your automation projects represents a paradigm shift in how businesses approach technology and innovation. It's about making the most of available resources, leveraging AI and no-code tools to automate processes, and empower teams. As we delve deeper into this chapter, we'll explore key tools and strategies for bootstrapping your automation efforts, providing practical insights and guidance to help you harness the power of these technologies. Whether you're a small business owner, a manager in a large corporation, or a solo entrepreneur, bootstrapping automation offers a pathway to enhanced efficiency, innovation, and competitive advantage. Let's embark on this journey together, exploring how you can transform your business with the power of AI and no-code automation.

Understanding AI and no-code Tools

In the journey of bootstrapping automation, grasping the essence of AI and no-code tools is akin to finding your compass and map—it equips you with the knowledge to navigate the vast landscape of technological possibilities. This segment delves into the core of AI and no-code tools, shedding light on their functionalities, benefits, and the transformative potential they hold for businesses eager to embrace automation without the hefty price tag or complex coding.

What are AI and no-code Tools?

AI and no-code tools are the linchpins of modern automation, enabling businesses to streamline operations, enhance productivity, and foster innovation with unprecedented ease and speed.

- AI Tools: These are applications or platforms that leverage artificial intelligence to perform tasks, analyze data, or make decisions that would typically require human intelligence. They can range from simple chatbots to sophisticated predictive analytics systems, all designed to operate with varying degrees of autonomy and complexity.

- no-code Tools: no-code platforms empower users to create software applications, automate workflows, or build databases without any programming knowledge. They feature intuitive, graphical interfaces where users can drag and drop components, set up rules, and design processes to suit their specific needs.

The Synergy of AI and no-code

When AI meets no-code, the result is a powerful synergy that democratizes technology, making it accessible to a broader audience. This combination allows users to:

- Automate Intelligently: Integrate AI functionalities into no-code applications to automate complex tasks, analyze data patterns, or enhance decision-making processes, all without delving into the intricacies of code.

- Innovate Rapidly: Quickly prototype and deploy AIdriven solutions, test new ideas, and iterate based on feedback, all within a no-code environment that encourages experimentation and agility.

- Empower Teams: Enable individuals across your organization, regardless of their technical expertise, to contribute to automation and innovation efforts, fostering a culture of collaboration and continuous improvement.

Key Features of AI and no-code Tools

To truly leverage the power of AI and no-code tools, it's essential to understand their key features and how they can be applied to your business processes:

- userf-riendly Interfaces: no-code platforms are designed with simplicity in mind, featuring drag-and-drop builders, preconfigured templates, and visual workflows that make technology development intuitive and accessible.

- AI Capabilities: Modern no-code tools often come equipped with AI functionalities, such as natural language processing, image recognition, or machine learning, allowing users to incorporate advanced technologies into their solutions effortlessly.

- Integration Options: Many no-code platforms offer extensive integration capabilities, enabling you to connect various applications, data sources, and services to create cohesive and automated workflows.

- Scalability: As your business grows, your no-code and AI solutions can scale with you, accommodating increased demand, more complex processes, or additional data without requiring a complete overhaul of your existing systems.

Benefits of Using AI and no-code Tools

The advantages of adopting AI and no-code tools are manifold, offering businesses the opportunity to:

- Reduce Development Costs: Eliminate the need for expensive software development projects or specialized programming expertise, significantly lowering the barrier to entry for automation and innovation.

- Accelerate TimetoMarket: Quickly design, test, and deploy automated solutions, enabling your business to respond swiftly to market changes, customer needs, or competitive pressures.

- Enhance Operational Efficiency: Automate routine tasks, streamline workflows, and improve data accuracy, freeing up your team to focus on strategic initiatives and core business activities.

- **Drive Business Innovation:** Foster a culture of innovation by empowering employees to create and implement AI driven solutions, encouraging a proactive approach to problem-solving and process improvement.

Understanding AI and no-code tools is the first step toward unlocking their potential to transform your business. By embracing these technologies, you can bootstrap your automation efforts, making sophisticated solutions not only achievable but also affordable and manageable. In the following sections, we'll explore specific tools and platforms that exemplify these principles, providing you with practical insights and guidance to embark on your own bootstrapping automation journey.

Key Tools for Bootstrapping Automation

In the dynamic world of AI automation, having a suite of versatile and powerful tools at your disposal can significantly streamline your processes and enhance your business's operational efficiency. This segment delves into an array of essential tools that are pivotal for bootstrapping automation, offering insights into their functionalities and practical applications.

Airtable

- **Overview:** Airtable merges the simplicity of spreadsheet use with the complexity of a robust database, providing a versatile platform for organizing, tracking, and managing data with ease.

- Use Cases: Ideal for project management, CRM, inventory tracking, and event planning, Airtable's customizable views and rich automation features enable businesses to streamline their operations and foster collaboration.

ChatGPT

- Overview: ChatGPT, powered by OpenAI, is an advanced language model that can generate humanlike text, providing businesses with a powerful tool for automating customer service, content creation, and more.

- Use Cases: Implement ChatGPT to enhance chatbot interactions, generate creative content, or even automate email responses, providing timely and contextually relevant communication.

Crowd AI

- Overview: Crowd AI offers a platform that enables users to build custom AI models without requiring deep technical expertise, focusing on image recognition and analysis.

- Use Cases: Utilize Crowd AI to analyze aerial imagery for urban planning, detect anomalies in manufacturing processes, or enhance retail experiences through image-based customer insights.

ObviouslyAI

- Overview: ObviouslyAI is a no-code tool that empowers users to build and deploy machine learning models quickly, focusing on predictive analytics without the need for data science background.

- Use Cases: Predict customer churn, forecast sales, or optimize marketing campaigns using intuitive, data-driven models that can be built and iterated rapidly.

Zapier

- Overview: Zapier stands out for its ability to connect and automate workflows across thousands of apps, enabling businesses to create complex automation sequences without coding.

- Use Cases: Automate data entry, synchronize information across platforms, or set up automated alerts and notifications to streamline communication and operational processes.

Azure AI

- Overview: Azure AI is a set of cloud-based services that provide powerful AI capabilities, including machine learning, knowledge mining, and cognitive services.

- Use Cases: Develop custom AI solutions, enhance business analytics, or create intelligent applications that can see, hear, speak, understand, and interpret user needs.

DataRobot, Inc.

- Overview: DataRobot offers an enterprise AI platform that automates the process of building, deploying, and managing machine learning models.

- Use Cases: Accelerate decision-making processes, enhance predictive analytics, and optimize business outcomes across various domains like finance, healthcare, and marketing.

Akkio Inc.

- Overview: Akkio focuses on making AI and machine learning accessible to nontechnical users, allowing for rapid model development and deployment.

- Use Cases: Streamline risk assessment, customer segmentation, or any data-driven decision-making process, leveraging AI to extract insights and automate evaluations.

Google AutoML

- Overview: Google AutoML enables users to train high-quality custom machine learning models with minimal effort and machine learning expertise.

- Use Cases: Create models tailored to your business needs, whether for image recognition, language translation, or sentiment analysis, enhancing automation and intelligence.

Lobe

- Overview: Lobe is a userf-riendly tool from Microsoft that simplifies the process of building, training, and exporting custom machine learning models, focusing on visual interfaces.

- Use Cases: Develop AI models to classify images, recognize gestures, or analyze text, integrating them into applications to automate and enhance user experiences.

Make (formerly Integromat)

- Overview: Make provides a visual platform for automating workflows across various applications and services, enabling complex data manipulations and integrations.

- Use Cases: Connect disparate systems to automate data transfers, streamline approvals, or synchronize information across platforms, reducing manual intervention.

N8n

- Overview: N8n is an extendable workflow automation tool that offers a node-based approach to creating automated processes, supporting a wide range of integrations.

- Use Cases: Automate content updates, manage event triggers, or synchronize data across tools, customizing workflows to fit specific business requirements.

Nanonets

- Overview: Nanonets leverage AI to offer advanced OCR and machine learning capabilities, simplifying the process of extracting and interpreting data from various formats.

- Use Cases: Automate document processing, data extraction from images or PDFs, and streamline data entry tasks, enhancing accuracy and efficiency.

Alter AI

- Overview: Alter AI provides tools to automate repetitive tasks using AI, focusing on simplifying complex processes and reducing manual workload.

- Use Cases: Implement AI assistants for data entry, automate customer support queries, or optimize backend processes, freeing up resources for strategic tasks.

Amazon SageMaker

- Overview: Amazon SageMaker is a fully managed service that enables developers and data scientists to build, train, and deploy machine learning models quickly.

- Use Cases: Enhance business analytics, develop predictive models, or create personalized user experiences, leveraging Amazon's extensive cloud infrastructure.

Apple Create ML

- Overview: Apple Create ML is a userf-riendly tool that allows developers to train and deploy machine learning models on Apple devices, utilizing an intuitive interface.

- Use Cases: Develop apps with integrated machine learning features, such as image classification, natural language processing, or style transfer, enhancing user engagement.

Bravo

- Overview: Bravo is a no-code tool that transforms your design files into fully functional mobile applications, bridging the gap between design and development.

- Use Cases: Create custom mobile apps from design prototypes, integrate with backend services, or develop interactive user interfaces without deep coding knowledge.

Toddle.dev

- Overview: Toddle.dev is an innovative no-code platform that simplifies the creation of web applications, allowing users to design, build, and launch applications without any coding knowledge.

- Use Cases: Ideal for developing prototypes, internal business tools, ecommerce sites, and marketing landing pages, Toddle.dev empowers a wide range of professionals to bring their digital visions to life efficiently.

Builder

- Overview: Builder is a no-code platform that empowers teams to build, publish, and test digital experiences without relying on developers.

- Use Cases: Design and deploy websites, ecommerce platforms, or marketing landing pages, utilizing AI-driven suggestions to optimize performance and user engagement.

Softr

- Overview: Soft is a no-code platform designed to streamline app development, offering a range of customization options and integrations.

- Use Cases: Build and iterate web or mobile applications rapidly, customize user experiences, or integrate with existing systems to enhance functionality and automation.

Cogniflow

- Overview: Cogniflow allows users to create AI models from text or images without coding, making AI more accessible and applicable across various domains.

- Use Cases: Automate content categorization, enhance image-based analyses, or develop AI-driven insights, applying models to real-world business challenges.

Google Teachable Machine

- Overview: Google Teachable Machine is an easy-to-use tool that enables users to create machine learning models based on their own data, fostering experimentation and learning.

- Use Cases: Develop custom models to recognize images, sounds, or poses, integrating them into educational tools, interactive projects, or business solutions.

GPT Appstore

- Overview: GPT Appstore harnesses the power of generative AI, offering a platform for discovering and deploying AIdriven applications across various functions.

- Use Cases: Explore and implement AI applications for content generation, data analysis, or process automation, tapping into a growing ecosystem of AI solutions.

Jasper

- Overview: Jasper is an AIpowered content creation tool that assists in generating high-quality written content, streamlining the content development process.

- Use Cases: Enhance marketing efforts with automated content creation for blogs, social media, or advertising copy, maintaining consistency and engaging audiences.

Mailchimp

- **Overview:** Mailchimp is a renowned marketing automation platform that integrates AI to optimize campaigns, analyze performance, and personalize communications.

- **Use Cases:** Automate email campaigns, segment audiences based on behavior, or test different marketing strategies, leveraging AI to maximize engagement and ROI.

Levity

- **Overview:** Levity is an AI tool designed to automate data classification and processing, enabling businesses to handle information more efficiently and accurately.

- **Use Cases:** Streamline data categorization, automate content moderation, or enhance customer feedback analysis, applying AI to improve data handling and insights.

AIPRM

- **Overview:** AIPRM is a pioneering platform designed to enhance the capabilities of AI models, particularly ChatGPT, by providing a suite of tools that enable users to create, share, and utilize prompts more effectively, optimizing the AI's performance for specific tasks.

- Use Cases: Ideal for businesses and individuals looking to harness the full potential of AI in areas like content creation, customer service, and data analysis, AIPRM streamlines the process of generating precise and contextually relevant AI outputs, thereby maximizing efficiency and productivity.

The list goes on. Every day, there's a new app. (For examples of AI tools, mostly built on no-code platforms, https://www.futuretools.io is a good resource.)

By integrating these tools into your business processes, you can unlock new levels of efficiency, creativity, and innovation, propelling your organization forward in the digital age.

Whether you're automating routine tasks, developing custom applications, or harnessing AI for data analysis, the key is to select the tools that align with your goals and empower your team to achieve more with less.

www.ingramcontent.com/pod-product-compliance
Lightning Source LLC
Chambersburg PA
CBHW050319230526
45471CB00005B/2259